Winfield Public School
OS150 Park Street
Winfield, IL 60190

Kevin's Kwanzaa

Lisa Bullard

illustrated by **Constanza Basaluzzo**

M MILLBROOK PRESS · MINNEAPOLIS

For the LaPatka Family —L.B.
For Lourdes and Ramiro —C.B.

Millbrook Press
A division of Lerner Publishing Group, Inc.
241 First Avenue North
Minneapolis, MN 55401 USA

For reading levels and more information, look up this title at
www.lernerbooks.com.

Main body text set in Slappy Inline 18/28.
Typeface provided by T26.

Library of Congress Cataloging-in-Publication Data

Bullard, Lisa.
    Kevin's Kwanzaa / by Lisa Bullard ; illustrated by Constanza
Basaluzzo.
       p.   cm. — (Cloverleaf books—Fall and winter holidays)
    Includes index.
    Summary: Kevin is excited for his turn to light the candles
on the last night of Kwanzaa. As he narrates through the
week of Kwanzaa, readers learn about the origins, purpose,
and rituals of this holiday.
    ISBN 978-0-7613-5075-0 (lib. bdg. : alk. paper)
    ISBN 978-1-4677-0124-2 (eb pdf)
    1. Kwanzaa—Juvenile literature. 2. African Americans—
Social life and customs—Juvenile literature. I. Basaluzzo,
Constanza. II. Title.
GT4403.B85 2013
394.2612—dc23   2011044857

Manufactured in the United States of America
4-47047-10786-12/21/2018

TABLE OF CONTENTS

Chapter One

Ready for Kwanzaa

Hi! I'm Kevin. See the decorations I'm making? We're getting ready for **Kwanzaa.**

That's a special holiday for my family. Mom says it celebrates our African American culture.

Long ago, many Africans were forced to come to the United States. They came as slaves. Slaves had very hard lives. The Civil War ended slavery in the United States in 1865. But sometimes, African Americans have still been treated unfairly. Kwanzaa is a way for them to come together. They celebrate their shared African culture.

Mom puts a **mat** on a table. I add the **candleholder** and **candles**. Mom adds fruits and vegetables. There's an **ear of corn** for each kid.

The Kwanzaa holiday began in the United States. But parts of it come from old African celebrations. These celebrations were held when the crops were ready. The fruits and vegetables remind people of this.

Next comes the **UNITY CUP**. Didn't I do a great job decorating it? We put out presents too!

Now we're ready for Kwanzaa.

Chapter Two

Lighting the Candles

Kwanzaa lasts for **seven days**, from December 26 until January 1. We light another candle each night.

I can hardly wait for my turn! It's on the last night. Grandpa goes first. Tonight he lights the **black candle.**

The candleholder has three red candles, three green candles, and one black candle. The candles are lit in a special order.

Then Grandpa explains the Kwanzaa word for the first day. Every day has a special word in **Swahili.** That's an African language.

The word *Kwanzaa* also comes from Swahili.

Nguzo Saba
The Seven Principles

Umoja = Unity

Kujichagulia = Self-Determination

Ujima = Collective Work and Responsibility

Ujamaa = Cooperative Economics

Nia = Purpose

Kuumba = Creativity

Imani = Faith

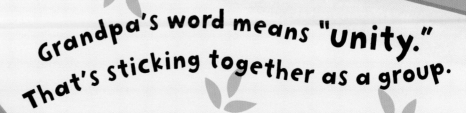

Grandpa's word means "Unity." That's sticking together as a group.

Grandpa says **sticking together** is why Kwanzaa began. A man named Dr. Maulana Karenga created Kwanzaa in 1966.

Many people have worked to make the lives of African Americans better. Lots of important work took place in the 1950s and the 1960s. Dr. Karenga created Kwanzaa during this time.

He wanted to bring African Americans together. He wanted them to feel proud of their shared African background.

I guess it worked, because I sure feel **proud!**

Chapter Three

Another Word Each Night

Somebody else lights the candles each night. I want to be ready for my turn. So I watch closely.

Families might also share other activities each night of Kwanzaa. Some families have everyone drink water or juice from the unity cup.

Mom lights the candles on the third night. We talk about helping one another **solve problems**. Mom says maybe we can work together on my messy bedroom problem.

My brother lights the candles on the fifth night. We talk about **setting goals to help our community.**

Right now I have two goals. I want to grow up to be a teacher. And I want to light the **Kwanzaa candles!**

Most people who celebrate Kwanzaa live in the United States. They are part of the African American community. But people in other countries also celebrate. They usually come from an African background.

The sixth night of Kwanzaa is my favorite.
We go to a big party every year.

The word for the sixth day means "creativity." Creativity is an important part of Kwanzaa. People make their own decorations. They make Kwanzaa presents for one another.

I **boom, boom** with the drummers.
I **stomp, stomp** with the dancers.

I eat and eat!

Chapter Four

Finally, My Turn

It's the last day of Kwanzaa. I like opening my presents. But I like lighting the candles even more!

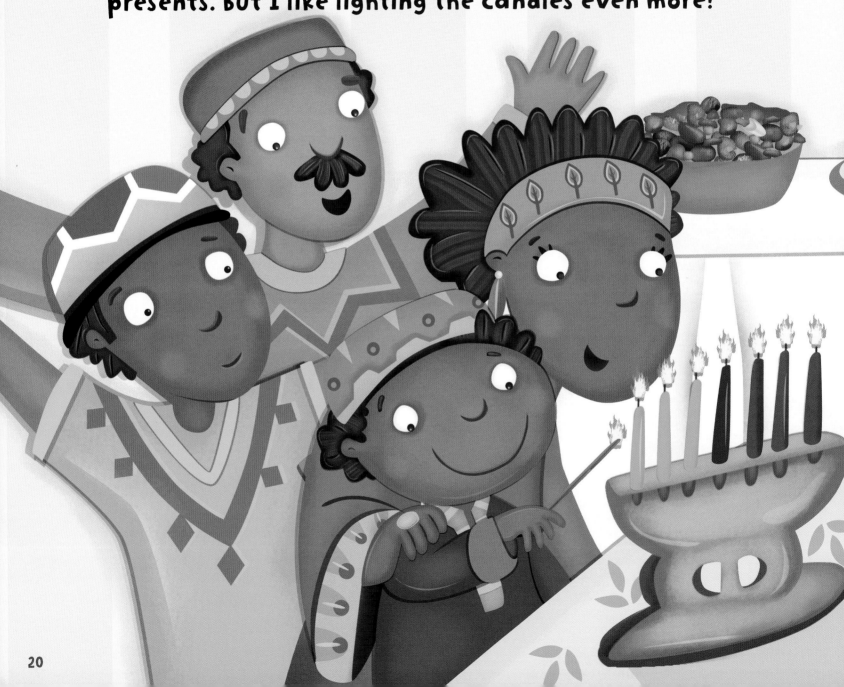

Grandpa says my special word means **"faith."** He says I should believe in our people every day.

Nguzo Saba
The Seven Principles

Umoja = Unity

Kujichagulia = Self-Determinati

Ujima = Collective Work and Responsibility

Ujamaa = Cooperative Econor

Nia = Purpose

Kuumba = Creativity

ni = Faith

That will be like living **Kwanzaa** all year long!

Make a Kwanzaa Drum

Creativity is an important part of the Kwanzaa celebration. You can use your creativity to make a Kwanzaa drum!

What you will need:

A round 18 oz. oatmeal container (empty)
Transparent tape
Glue stick
Pencil
Scissors

Ruler
Black marker
1 sheet of black construction paper (9"x12")
½ sheet of green construction paper (9"x6")
½ sheet of red construction paper (9"x6")

How to make your drum:

1) Set the lid of your container on the red paper. Trace around the outside of the lid with your pencil. Put the lid back on the container.

2) Cut out the circle that you have created. Put several pieces of tape around the circle. The ends of the tape should stick off the edges of the circle so that they look like the rays of a sun.

3) Set the red circle on top of the lid. Push down the pieces of tape so that the circle is taped onto the container.

4) On the short edge of the black paper, use the ruler to measure the 7-inch point. Make a pencil mark. Starting at this mark, draw a straight line across the paper using the edge of the ruler. Cut all along the line.

5) Glue the bigger piece of black paper around the container the tall way. There will be a thin strip that is not covered by the paper.

6) Use the ruler and your pencil to measure a strip in the green paper that is 1 inch wide and 7 inches long. Cut out the strip. Use the black marker to write "Kwanzaa" along this strip.

7) Glue this green strip on so that it runs up and down the side of the container. It should cover the section of the container that is not yet covered by black paper.

GLOSSARY

African American: someone or something that has both an African and an American background

candleholder: something that is made to hold candles

celebration: an event to show how special or important something or someone is

creativity: ability to make something using one's imagination

culture: shared beliefs, practices, language, foods, and other things that define a group of people

decoration: something added to make a thing look pretty or special

Kwanzaa (KWAHN-zah): a holiday that celebrates African Americans. The word comes from the Swahili word *kwanza.*

slave: a person who is owned by another person and is forced to work without pay

Swahili (swah-HEE-lee): an African language spoken in Tanzania, Kenya, Uganda, and other countries

unity: the quality of working together as one

BOOKS

Otto, Carolyn. *Celebrate Kwanzaa: With Candles, Community, and the Fruits of the Harvest.* Washington, DC: National Geographic, 2008.
Bright photos show some of the special ways Kwanzaa is celebrated.

Ross, Kathy. *All New Crafts for Kwanzaa.* Minneapolis: Millbrook Press, 2007.
This book shows you how to make many different Kwanzaa crafts.

Tokunbo, Dimitrea. *The Sound of Kwanzaa.* New York: Scholastic, 2009.
Learn more about the meaning of Kwanzaa by exploring the sounds of this seven-day celebration.

WEBSITES

Africa for Kids
http://pbskids.org/africa/
Find out more about Africa through a story and activities on this website from PBS Kids Go!

Celebrate!
http://pbskids.org/arthur/holiday/scrapbook/kwaa1.html
Follow along as Arthur's friend the Brain celebrates Kwanzaa at this website from PBS Kids Go!

Light the Kwanzaa Candles
http://www.imgag.com/product/full/ap/3029536/
Visit this website and light each of the Kwanzaa candles while you learn the meaning of each day of Kwanzaa.

LERNER ✐ SOURCE™
Expand learning beyond the printed book. Download free, complementary educational resources for this book from our website, www.lernersource.com.